Cabled BABY Blankets

by Bonnie Bark…

Classic cables and other Aran patterns bring … Barker's four baby blankets. Their sweet little size is ideal for everyday use.

Designer's Dedication
To my five precious babies…Becky, Caleb, Hannah, Hudson, and Joseph.

He will tend His flock like a shepherd;
He will gather the lambs in His arms;
He will carry them in His bosom,
and gently lead those that are with young.
— Isaiah 40:11

LEISURE ARTS, INC.
Maumelle, Arkansas

Aran Appeal

INTERMEDIATE

Finished Size: 26½" x 29" (67.5 cm x 73.5 cm)

SHOPPING LIST

Yarn (Medium Weight) MEDIUM 4

[16 ounces, 1,020 yards

(454 grams, 932 meters) per skein**]**:

☐ One skein

Crochet Hooks

☐ Size K (6.5 mm) **and**

☐ Size I (5.5 mm)

or sizes needed for gauge

GAUGE INFORMATION

With larger size hook, in pattern, (sc, ch 1, dc) 5 times (15 sts) and 10 rows = 4" (10 cm)

Gauge Swatch: 4½"w x 4"h (11.5 cm x 10 cm)

With larger size hook, ch 18.

Row 1: Sc in second ch from hook and in each ch across: 17 sc.

Row 2: Ch 2 **(counts as first hdc, now and throughout)**, turn; ★ (sc, ch 1, dc) in next sc, skip next 2 sc; repeat from ★ 4 times **more**, sc in last sc: 17 sts.

Rows 3-10: Ch 2, turn; skip next dc, (sc, ch 1, dc) in next ch-1 sp, ★ skip next 2 sts, (sc, ch 1, dc) in next ch-1 sp; repeat from ★ 3 times **more**, skip next sc, sc in last hdc.

Finish off.

STITCH GUIDE

FRONT POST DOUBLE CROCHET *(abbreviated FPdc)*

YO, insert hook from **front** to **back** around post of st indicated ***(Fig. 2, page 31)***, YO and pull up a loop (3 loops on hook), (YO and draw through 2 loops on hook) twice.

BACK POST DOUBLE CROCHET *(abbreviated BPdc)*

YO, insert hook from **back** to **front** around post of st indicated ***(Fig. 2, page 31)***, YO and pull up a loop (3 loops on hook), (YO and draw through 2 loops on hook) twice.

FRONT POST TREBLE CROCHET *(abbreviated FPtr)*

YO twice, insert hook from **front** to **back** around post of st indicated ***(Fig. 2, page 31)***, YO and pull up a loop (4 loops on hook), (YO and draw through 2 loops on hook) 3 times.

BODY

With larger size hook, ch 92.

Row 1 (Right side)**:** Sc in second ch from hook and in each ch across: 91 sc.

Row 2: Ch 2 **(counts as first hdc, now and throughout Body)**, turn; **[**(sc, ch 1, dc) in next sc, skip next 2 sc**]** 12 times, hdc in next sc, (dc in next 3 sc, hdc in next sc) 4 times, **[**(sc, ch 1, dc) in next sc, skip next 2 sc**]** 12 times, sc in last sc: 67 sts and 24 ch-1 sps.

Row 3: Ch 2, turn; skip next dc, (sc, ch 1, dc) in next ch-1 sp, **[**skip next 2 sts, (sc, ch 1, dc) in next ch-1 sp**]** 11 times, skip next sc, hdc in next hdc, (work FPdc around each of next 3 sts, hdc in next hdc) 4 times, skip next dc, (sc, ch 1, dc) in next ch-1 sp, **[**skip next 2 sts, (sc, ch 1, dc) in next ch-1 sp**]** 11 times, skip next sc, sc in last hdc.

Row 4: Ch 2, turn; skip next dc, (sc, ch 1, dc) in next ch-1 sp, **[**skip next 2 sts, (sc, ch 1, dc) in next ch-1 sp**]** 11 times, skip next sc, hdc in next hdc, (work BPdc around each of next 3 sts, hdc in next hdc) 4 times, skip next dc, (sc, ch 1, dc) in next ch-1 sp, **[**skip next 2 sts, (sc, ch 1, dc) in next ch-1 sp**]** 11 times, skip next sc, sc in last hdc.

Row 5: Ch 2, turn; skip next dc, (sc, ch 1, dc) in next ch-1 sp, **[**skip next 2 sts, (sc, ch 1, dc) in next ch-1 sp**]** 11 times, skip next sc, hdc in next hdc, skip next 3 sts, hdc in next hdc, work FPtr around each of next 3 sts, working **behind** last 4 sts made, work FPtr around each of 3 skipped sts, hdc in next hdc, skip next 3 sts, hdc in next hdc, work FPtr around each of next 3 sts, working in **front** of last 4 sts made, work FPtr around each of 3 skipped sts, hdc in next hdc, skip next dc, (sc, ch 1, dc) in next ch-1 sp, **[**skip next 2 sts, (sc, ch 1, dc) in next ch-1 sp**]** 11 times, skip next sc, sc in last hdc.

Row 6: Ch 2, turn; skip next dc, (sc, ch 1, dc) in next ch-1 sp, **[**skip next 2 sts, (sc, ch 1, dc) in next ch-1 sp**]** 11 times, skip next sc, hdc in next hdc, ★ work BPdc around each of next 3 sts, hdc in sp **before** next st ***(Fig. 3, page 31)***, work BPdc around each of next 3 sts, skip next hdc, hdc in next hdc; repeat from ★ once **more**, skip next dc, (sc, ch 1, dc) in next ch-1 sp, **[**skip next 2 sts, (sc, ch 1, dc) in next ch-1 sp**]** 11 times, skip next sc, sc in last hdc.

Rows 7-64: Repeat Rows 3-6, 14 times; then repeat Rows 3 and 4 once **more**.

Do **not** finish off.

EDGING

Change to smaller size hook.

Rnd 1 (Right side)**:** Ch 1, turn; sc in first sc, [skip next dc, 2 sc in next ch-1 sp, sc in next sc] 12 times, sc in next 17 sts, [skip next dc, 2 sc in next ch-1 sp, sc in next sc] 12 times, sc in last hdc, ch 2 (corner sp); † working in end of rows, sc in first 2 rows, (2 sc in next row, sc in next row) across, ch 2 †; working in free loops of beginning ch ***(Fig. 1, page 31)***, sc in each ch across, ch 2, repeat from † to † once; join with slip st to first sc: 372 sc and 4 corner ch-2 sps.

Rnd 2: Ch 2 **(does not count as a st)**, do **not** turn; dc in first sc and in each sc across to next corner ch-2 sp, 8 dc in corner ch-2 sp, ★ dc in next sc and in each sc across to next corner ch-2 sp, 8 dc in corner ch-2 sp; repeat from ★ 2 times **more**; join with slip st to first dc: 404 dc.

Rnd 3: Ch 2, work FPdc around first dc, work BPdc around next dc, (work FPdc around next dc, work BPdc around next dc) around; join with slip st to first FPdc.

Rnds 4 and 5: Ch 2, work FPdc around first FPdc, work BPdc around next BPdc, (work FPdc around next FPdc, work BPdc around next BPdc) around; join with slip st to first FPdc.

Finish off.

Bold Cables

●●●○

INTERMEDIATE

Finished Size: 25" x 27½" (63.5 cm x 70 cm)

SHOPPING LIST

Yarn (Medium Weight) MEDIUM 4

[16 ounces, 1,020 yards

(454 grams, 932 meters) per skein**]**:

- ☐ One skein

Crochet Hooks

- ☐ Size K (6.5 mm) **and**
- ☐ Size I (5.5 mm)

  or sizes needed for gauge

GAUGE INFORMATION

With larger size hook, in pattern, (sc, ch 1, dc) 5 times (15 sts) and 10 rows = 4" (10 cm)

Gauge Swatch: 4½"w x 4"h (11.5 cm x 10 cm)

With larger size hook, ch 18.

Row 1: Sc in second ch from hook and in each ch across: 17 sc.

Row 2: Ch 2 **(counts as first hdc, now and throughout)**, turn; ★ (sc, ch 1, dc) in next sc, skip next 2 sc; repeat from ★ 4 times **more**, sc in last sc: 17 sts.

Rows 3-10: Ch 2, turn; skip next dc, (sc, ch 1, dc) in next ch-1 sp, ★ skip next 2 sts, (sc, ch 1, dc) in next ch-1 sp; repeat from ★ 3 times **more**, skip next sc, sc in last hdc.

Finish off.

STITCH GUIDE

FRONT POST DOUBLE CROCHET *(abbreviated FPdc)*

YO, insert hook from **front** to **back** around post of st indicated ***(Fig. 2, page 31)***, YO and pull up a loop (3 loops on hook), (YO and draw through 2 loops on hook) twice.

BACK POST DOUBLE CROCHET *(abbreviated BPdc)*

YO, insert hook from **back** to **front** around post of st indicated ***(Fig. 2, page 31)***, YO and pull up a loop (3 loops on hook), (YO and draw through 2 loops on hook) twice.

FRONT POST TREBLE CROCHET *(abbreviated FPtr)*

YO twice, insert hook from **front** to **back** around post of st indicated ***(Fig. 2, page 31)***, YO and pull up a loop (4 loops on hook), (YO and draw through 2 loops on hook) 3 times.

BODY

With larger size hook, ch 86.

Row 1 (Right side): Sc in second ch from hook and in each ch across: 85 sc.

Row 2: Ch 2 **(counts as first hdc, now and throughout Body)**, turn; (sc, ch 1, dc) in first sc, skip next 2 sc, (sc, ch 1, dc) in next sc, skip next 2 sc, hdc in next sc, (dc in next 3 sc, hdc in next sc) twice, ★ **[**(sc, ch 1, dc) in next sc, skip next 2 sc**]** 4 times, hdc in next sc, (dc in next 3 sc, hdc in next sc) twice; repeat from ★ 2 times **more**, **[**(sc, ch 1, dc) in next sc, skip next 2 sc**]** twice, sc in last sc: 70 sts and 16 ch-1 sps.

Row 3: Ch 2, turn; skip next dc, (sc, ch 1, dc) in next ch-1 sp, skip next 2 sts, (sc, ch 1, dc) in next ch-1 sp, skip next sc, hdc in next hdc, (work FPdc around each of next 3 sts, hdc in next hdc) twice, ★ skip next dc, (sc, ch 1, dc) in next ch-1 sp, **[**skip next 2 sts, (sc, ch 1, dc) in next ch-1 sp**]** 3 times, skip next sc, hdc in next hdc, (work FPdc around each of next 3 sts, hdc in next hdc) twice; repeat from ★ 2 times **more**, skip next dc, (sc, ch 1, dc) in next ch-1 sp, skip next 2 sts, (sc, ch 1, dc) in next ch-1 sp, skip next sc, sc in last hdc.

Row 4: Ch 2, turn; skip next dc, (sc, ch 1, dc) in next ch-1 sp, skip next 2 sts, (sc, ch 1, dc) in next ch-1 sp, skip next sc, hdc in next hdc, (work BPdc around each of next 3 sts, hdc in next hdc) twice, ★ skip next dc, (sc, ch 1, dc) in next ch-1 sp, **[**skip next 2 sts, (sc, ch 1, dc) in next ch-1 sp**]** 3 times, skip next sc, hdc in next hdc, (work BPdc around each of next 3 sts, hdc in next hdc) twice; repeat from ★ 2 times **more**, skip next dc, (sc, ch 1, dc) in next ch-1 sp, skip next 2 sts, (sc, ch 1, dc) in next ch-1 sp, skip next sc, sc in last hdc.

Rows 5 and 6: Repeat Rows 3 and 4.

Row 7: Ch 2, turn; skip next dc, (sc, ch 1, dc) in next ch-1 sp, skip next 2 sts, (sc, ch 1, dc) in next ch-1 sp, skip next sc, hdc in next hdc, skip next 3 sts, hdc in next hdc, work FPtr around each of next 3 sts, working in **front** of last 4 sts made, work FPtr around each of 3 skipped sts, hdc in next hdc, ★ skip next dc, (sc, ch 1, dc) in next ch-1 sp, **[**skip next 2 sts, (sc, ch 1, dc) in next ch-1 sp**]** 3 times, skip next sc, hdc in next hdc, skip next 3 sts, hdc in next hdc, work FPtr around each of next 3 sts, working in **front** of last 4 sts made, work FPtr around each of 3 skipped sts, hdc in next hdc; repeat from ★ 2 times **more**, skip next dc, (sc, ch 1, dc) in next ch-1 sp, skip next 2 sts, (sc, ch 1, dc) in next ch-1 sp, skip next sc, sc in last hdc.

Row 8: Ch 2, turn; skip next dc, (sc, ch 1, dc) in next ch-1 sp, skip next 2 sts, (sc, ch 1, dc) in next ch-1 sp, skip next sc, hdc in next hdc, work BPdc around each of next 3 sts, hdc in sp **before** next st ***(Fig. 3, page 31)***, work BPdc around each of next 3 sts, skip next hdc, hdc in next hdc, ★ skip next dc, (sc, ch 1, dc) in next ch-1 sp, **[**skip next 2 sts, (sc, ch 1, dc) in next ch-1 sp**]** 3 times, skip next sc, hdc in next hdc, work BPdc around each of next 3 sts, hdc in sp **before** next st, work BPdc around each of next 3 sts, skip next hdc, hdc in next hdc; repeat from ★ 2 times **more**, skip next dc, (sc, ch 1, dc) in next ch-1 sp, skip next 2 sts, (sc, ch 1, dc) in next ch-1 sp, skip next sc, sc in last hdc.

Rows 9-60: Repeat Rows 3-8, 8 times; then repeat Rows 3-6 once **more**.

Do **not** finish off.

EDGING

Change to smaller size hook.

Rnd 1 (Right side)**:** Ch 1, turn; skip first 2 sts, 2 sc in next ch-1 sp, sc in next sc, skip next dc, 2 sc in next ch-1 sp, sc in next 10 sts, ★ skip next dc, 2 sc in next ch-1 sp, (sc in next sc, skip next dc, 2 sc in next ch-1 sp) 3 times, sc in next 10 sts; repeat from ★ 2 times **more**, (skip next dc, 2 sc in next ch-1 sp, sc in next sc) twice, sc in last hdc, ch 2 (corner sp); † working in end of rows, sc in first 2 rows, (2 sc in next row, sc in next row) across, ch 2 †; working in free loops of beginning ch ***(Fig. 1, page 31)***, sc in each ch across, ch 2; repeat from † to † once; join with slip st to first sc: 348 sc and 4 corner ch-2 sps.

Rnd 2: Ch 2 **(does not count as a st)**, do **not** turn; dc in first sc and in each sc across to next corner ch-2 sp, 8 dc in corner ch-2 sp, ★ dc in next sc and in each sc across to next corner ch-2 sp, 8 dc in corner ch-2 sp; repeat from ★ 2 times **more**; join with slip st to first dc: 380 dc.

Rnd 3: Ch 2, work FPdc around each of first 2 dc, work BPdc around each of next 2 dc, (work FPdc around each of next 2 dc, work BPdc around each of next 2 dc) around; join with slip st to first FPdc.

Rnds 4 and 5: Ch 2, work FPdc around each of first 2 FPdc, work BPdc around each of next 2 BPdc, (work FPdc around each of next 2 FPdc, work BPdc around each of next 2 BPdc) around; join with slip st to first FPdc.

Finish off.

Honeycomb

●●●○

INTERMEDIATE

Finished Size: 26" x 25" (66 cm x 63.5 cm)

SHOPPING LIST

Yarn (Medium Weight) MEDIUM 4

[16 ounces, 1,020 yards

(454 grams, 932 meters) per skein**]**:

- ☐ One skein

Crochet Hooks

- ☐ Size K (6.5 mm) **and**
- ☐ Size I (5.5 mm)

or sizes needed for gauge

GAUGE INFORMATION

With larger size hook, in rib pattern (Rows 1-6), 17 sts = 4$^1/_8$" (10.5 cm); 10 rows = 4" (10 cm)

Gauge Swatch: 4$^1/_8$"w x 4"h (10.5 cm x 10 cm)

With larger size hook, ch 19.

Row 1 (Right side): Dc in fourth ch from hook **(3 skipped chs count as first dc)** and in each ch across: 17 dc.

Row 2: Ch 2 **(counts as first hdc, now and throughout)**, turn; work FPdc around next st, (work BPdc around next st, work FPdc around next st) across to last st, hdc in last st.

Row 3: Ch 2, turn; work BPdc around next st, (work FPdc around next st, work BPdc around next st) across to last hdc, hdc in last hdc.

Rows 4-10: Repeat Rows 2 and 3, 3 times; then repeat Row 2 once **more**.

Finish off.

STITCH GUIDE

FRONT POST DOUBLE CROCHET *(abbreviated FPdc)*

YO, insert hook from **front** to **back** around post of st indicated ***(Fig. 2, page 31)***, YO and pull up a loop (3 loops on hook), (YO and draw through 2 loops on hook) twice.

BACK POST DOUBLE CROCHET *(abbreviated BPdc)*

YO, insert hook from **back** to **front** around post of st indicated ***(Fig. 2, page 31)***, YO and pull up a loop (3 loops on hook), (YO and draw through 2 loops on hook) twice.

FRONT POST TREBLE CROCHET *(abbreviated FPtr)*

YO twice, insert hook from **front** to **back** around post of st indicated ***(Fig. 2, page 31)***, YO and pull up a loop (4 loops on hook), (YO and draw through 2 loops on hook) 3 times.

BODY

With larger size hook, ch 109.

Row 1 (Right side): Dc in back ridge ***(Fig. A)*** of fourth ch from hook (**3 skipped chs count as first dc**) and each ch across: 107 dc.

Fig. A

Row 2: Ch 2 (**counts as first hdc, now and throughout**), turn; work FPdc around next dc, (work BPdc around next dc, work FPdc around next dc) across to last dc, hdc in last dc.

Row 3: Ch 2, turn; work BPdc around next st, (work FPdc around next st, work BPdc around next st) across to last hdc, hdc in last hdc.

Row 4: Ch 2, turn; work FPdc around next st, (work BPdc around next st, work FPdc around next st) across to last hdc, hdc in last hdc.

Rows 5 and 6: Repeat Rows 3 and 4.

Row 7: Ch 2, turn; (work BPdc around next st, work FPdc around next st) 5 times, † ★ skip next 2 sts, work FPdc around each of next 2 sts, working **behind** last 2 sts made, work FPdc around each of 2 skipped sts, skip next 2 sts, work FPdc around each of next 2 sts, working in **front** of last 2 sts made, work FPdc around each of 2 skipped sts; repeat from ★ 2 times **more** †, (work BPdc around next st, work FPdc around next st) 5 times, hdc in next st, (work FPdc around each of next 3 sts, hdc in next st) 4 times, (work FPdc around next st, work BPdc around next st) 5 times, repeat from † to † once, (work FPdc around next st, work BPdc around next st) 5 times, hdc in last hdc.

Row 8: Ch 2, turn; work FPdc around next st, (work BPdc around next st, work FPdc around next st) 4 times, work BPdc around each of next 25 sts, (work FPdc around next st, work BPdc around next st) 5 times, hdc in next hdc, (work BPdc around each of next 3 sts, hdc in next hdc) 4 times, (work BPdc around next st, work FPdc around next st) 5 times, work BPdc around each of next 25 sts, work FPdc around next st, (work BPdc around next st, work FPdc around next st) 4 times, hdc in last hdc.

Row 9: Ch 2, turn; (work BPdc around next st, work FPdc around next st) 5 times, † ★ skip next 2 sts, work FPdc around each of next 2 sts, working in **front** of last 2 sts made, work FPdc around each of 2 skipped sts, skip next 2 sts, work FPdc around each of next 2 sts, working **behind** last 2 sts made, work FPdc around each of 2 skipped sts; repeat from ★ 2 times **more** †, (work BPdc around next st, work FPdc around next st) 5 times, hdc in next hdc, skip next 3 sts, hdc in next hdc, work FPtr around each of next 3 sts, working **behind** last 4 sts made, work FPtr around each of 3 skipped sts, hdc in next hdc, skip next 3 sts, hdc in next hdc, work FPtr around each of next 3 sts, working in **front** of last 4 sts made, work FPtr around each of 3 skipped sts, hdc in next hdc, (work FPdc around next st, work BPdc around next st) 5 times, repeat from † to † once, (work FPdc around next st, work BPdc around next st) 5 times, hdc in last hdc.

Row 10: Ch 2, turn; work FPdc around next st, (work BPdc around next st, work FPdc around next st) 4 times, work BPdc around each of next 25 sts, (work FPdc around next st, work BPdc around next st) 5 times, hdc in next hdc, ★ work BPdc around each of next 3 sts, hdc in sp **before** next st ***(Fig. 3, page 31)***, work BPdc around each of next 3 sts, skip next hdc, hdc in next hdc; repeat from ★ once **more**, (work BPdc around next st, work FPdc around next st) 5 times, work BPdc around each of next 25 sts, work FPdc around next st, (work BPdc around next st, work FPdc around next st) 4 times, hdc in last hdc.

Rows 11 and 12: Repeat Rows 7 and 8.

Row 13: Ch 2, turn; (work BPdc around next st, work FPdc around next st) 5 times, † ★ skip next 2 sts, work FPdc around each of next 2 sts, working in **front** of last 2 sts made, work FPdc around each of 2 skipped sts, skip next 2 sts, work FPdc around each of next 2 sts, working **behind** last 2 sts made, work FPdc around each of 2 skipped sts; repeat from ★ 2 times **more** †, (work BPdc around next st, work FPdc around next st) 5 times, hdc in next hdc, (work FPdc around each of next 3 sts, hdc in next hdc) 4 times, (work FPdc around next st, work BPdc around next st) 5 times, repeat from † to † once, (work FPdc around next st, work BPdc around next st) 5 times, hdc in last hdc.

Row 14: Repeat Row 8.

Row 15: Ch 2, turn; (work BPdc around next st, work FPdc around next st) 5 times, † ★ skip next 2 sts, work FPdc around each of next 2 sts, working **behind** last 2 sts made, work FPdc around each of 2 skipped sts, skip next 2 sts, work FPdc around each of next 2 sts, working in **front** of last 2 sts made, work FPdc around each of 2 skipped sts; repeat from ★ 2 times **more** †, (work BPdc around next st, work FPdc around next st) 5 times, hdc in next hdc, skip next 3 sts, hdc in next hdc, work FPtr around each of next 3 sts, working in **front** of last 4 sts made, work FPtr around each of 3 skipped sts, hdc in next hdc, skip next 3 sts, hdc in next hdc, work FPtr around each of next 3 sts, working **behind** last 4 sts made, work FPtr around each of 3 skipped sts, hdc in next hdc, (work FPdc around next st, work BPdc around next st) 5 times, repeat from † to † once, (work FPdc around next st, work BPdc around next st) 5 times, hdc in last hdc.

Row 16: Repeat Row 10.

Row 17: Repeat Row 13.

Row 18: Repeat Row 8.

Row 19: Ch 2, turn; (work BPdc around next st, work FPdc around next st) 5 times, † ★ skip next 2 sts, work FPdc around each of next 2 sts, working **behind** last 2 sts made, work FPdc around each of 2 skipped sts, skip next 2 sts, work FPdc around each of next 2 sts, working in **front** of last 2 sts made, work FPdc around each of 2 skipped sts; repeat from ★ 2 times **more** †, (work BPdc around next st, work FPdc around next st) 5 times, hdc in next hdc, skip next 3 sts, hdc in next hdc, work FPtr around each of next 3 sts, working **behind** last 4 sts made, work FPtr around each of 3 skipped sts, hdc in next hdc, skip next 3 sts, hdc in next hdc, work FPtr around each of next 3 sts, working in **front** of last 4 sts made, work FPtr around each of 3 skipped sts, hdc in next hdc, (work FPdc around next st, work BPdc around next st) 5 times, repeat from † to † once, (work FPdc around next st, work BPdc around next st) 5 times, hdc in last hdc.

Row 20: Repeat Row 10.

Row 21: Repeat Row 13.

Row 22: Repeat Row 8.

Rows 23 and 24: Repeat Rows 7 and 8.

Row 25: Ch 2, turn; (work BPdc around next st, work FPdc around next st) 5 times, † ★ skip next 2 sts, work FPdc around each of next 2 sts, working in **front** of last 2 sts made, work FPdc around each of 2 skipped sts, skip next 2 sts, work FPdc around each of next 2 sts, working **behind** last 2 sts made, work FPdc around each of 2 skipped sts; repeat from ★ 2 times **more** †, (work BPdc around next st, work FPdc around next st) 5 times, hdc in next hdc, skip next 3 sts, hdc in next hdc, work FPtr around each of next 3 sts, working in **front** of last 4 sts made, work FPtr around each of 3 skipped sts, hdc in next hdc, skip next 3 sts, hdc in next hdc, work FPtr around each of next 3 sts, working **behind** last 4 sts made, work FPtr around each of 3 skipped sts, hdc in next hdc, (work FPdc around next st, work BPdc around next st) 5 times, repeat from † to † once, (work FPdc around next st, work BPdc around next st) 5 times, hdc in last hdc.

Row 26: Repeat Row 10.

Rows 27-58: Repeat Rows 7-26 once, then repeat Rows 7-18 once **more**.

Row 59: Ch 2, turn; work BPdc around next st, (work FPdc around next st, work BPdc around next st) across to last hdc, hdc in last hdc.

Row 60: Ch 2, turn; work FPdc around next st, (work BPdc around next st, work FPdc around next st) across to last hdc, hdc in last hdc.

Rows 61-63: Repeat Rows 59 and 60 once, then repeat Row 59 once **more**.

Change to smaller size hook.

Row 64: Turn; slip st in each st across; finish off.

Woven Treasure

●●●○

INTERMEDIATE

Finished Size: 29½" x 27½" (75 cm x 70 cm)

SHOPPING LIST

Yarn (Medium Weight) MEDIUM 4

[16 ounces, 1,020 yards

(454 grams, 932 meters) per skein**]**:

- ☐ One skein

Crochet Hooks

- ☐ Size K (6.5 mm) **and**
- ☐ Size I (5.5 mm)

  or sizes needed for gauge

Additional Supplies

- ☐ 3/8" (10 mm) wide Ribbon - 3 yards (2.75 meters)

GAUGE INFORMATION

With larger size hook, in pattern,

16 sts = 4¼" (10.75 cm);

8 rows = 4½" (11.5 cm)

Gauge Swatch: 3¾"w x 4½"h (9.5 cm x 11.5 cm)

With larger size hook, ch 16.

Row 1: Dc in fourth ch from hook **(3 skipped chs count as first dc)** and in each ch across: 14 dc.

Row 2 (Right side): Ch 3 **(counts as first dc, now and throughout)**, turn; ★ skip next 2 sts, work FPtr around each of next 2 sts, working in **front** of last 2 sts made, work FPtr around each of 2 skipped sts; repeat from ★ 2 times **more**, dc in last st.

Row 3: Ch 3, turn; work BPtr around each of next 2 sts, **[**skip next 2 sts, work BPtr around each of next 2 sts, working **behind** last 2 sts made, work BPtr around each of 2 skipped sts**]** 2 times, work BPtr around each of next 2 sts, dc in last st.

Rows 4-8: Repeat Rows 2 and 3 twice, then repeat Row 2 once **more**.

Finish off.

STITCH GUIDE

TREBLE CROCHET *(abbreviated tr)*

YO twice, insert hook in sp indicated, YO and pull up a loop (4 loops on hook), (YO and draw through 2 loops on hook) 3 times.

BACK POST DOUBLE CROCHET *(abbreviated BPdc)*

YO, insert hook from **back** to **front** around post of st indicated ***(Fig. 2, page 31)***, YO and pull up a loop (3 loops on hook), (YO and draw through 2 loops on hook) twice.

FRONT POST TREBLE CROCHET *(abbreviated FPtr)*

YO twice, insert hook from **front** to **back** around post of st indicated ***(Fig. 2, page 31)***, YO and pull up a loop (4 loops on hook), (YO and draw through 2 loops on hook) 3 times.

BACK POST TREBLE CROCHET ***(abbreviated BPtr)***

YO twice, insert hook from **back** to **front** around post of st indicated ***(Fig. 2, page 31)***, YO and pull up a loop (4 loops on hook), (YO and draw through 2 loops on hook) 3 times.

BODY

With larger size hook, ch 98; place marker in third ch from hook for Edging placement.

Row 1: Dc in fourth ch from hook **(3 skipped chs count as first dc)** and in each ch across: 96 dc.

Row 2 (Right side)**:** Ch 3 **(counts as first dc, now and throughout)**, turn; ★ † [skip next 2 sts, work FPtr around each of next 2 sts, working in **front** of last 2 sts made, work FPtr around each of 2 skipped sts] 6 times, dc in next dc †, skip next 3 sts, work FPtr around each of next 3 sts, working in **front** of last 3 sts made, work FPtr around each of 3 skipped sts, work FPtr around each of next 3 sts, dc in next dc; repeat from ★ once **more**, then repeat from † to † once.

Row 3: Ch 3, turn; ★ † work BPtr around each of next 2 sts, [skip next 2 sts, work BPtr around each of next 2 sts, working **behind** last 2 sts made, work BPtr around each of 2 skipped sts] 5 times, work BPtr around each of next 2 sts, dc in next dc †, skip next 3 sts, work BPtr around each of next 3 sts, working **behind** last 3 sts made, work BPtr around each of 3 skipped sts, work BPtr around each of next 3 sts, dc in next dc; repeat from ★ once **more**, then repeat from † to † once.

Rows 4-42: Repeat Rows 2 and 3, 19 times; then repeat Row 2 once **more**.

Row 43: Ch 2 **(counts as first hdc)**, turn; work BPdc around next st and each st across to last dc, hdc in last dc; do **not** finish off.

EDGING

Change to smaller size hook.

Rnd 1 (Right side)**:** Ch 1, turn; sc in each st across to last st, (sc, ch 2, sc) in last st; 2 sc in end of each row across; working in free loops of beginning ch ***(Fig. 1, page 31)***, (sc, ch 2, sc) in marked ch (remove marker), sc in each ch across to last ch, (sc, ch 2, sc) in last ch; 2 sc in end of each row across; sc in same st as first sc, ch 2; join with slip st to first sc: 368 sc and 4 corner ch-2 sps.

Rnd 2 (Eyelet rnd)**:** Do **not** turn; slip st in next sc, ch 4 **(counts as first dc plus ch 1)**, ★ (skip next sc, dc in next sc, ch 1) across to next corner ch-2 sp, (dc, ch 1) 3 times in corner sp; repeat from ★ around to last st, skip last st; join with slip st to first dc: 196 dc and 196 ch-1 sps.

Rnd 3: (Slip st, ch 4, 7 tr) in next ch-1 sp, skip next ch-1 sp, sc in next ch-1 sp, skip next ch-1 sp, ★ 8 tr in next ch-1 sp, skip next ch-1 sp, sc in next ch-1 sp, skip next ch-1 sp; repeat from ★ around; join with slip st to top of beginning ch-4, finish off.

Beginning at one corner, weave ribbon through Eyelet round; tie in a bow.

General Instructions

ABBREVIATIONS

BPdc	Back Post double crochet(s)
BPtr	Back Post treble crochet(s)
ch(s)	chain(s)
cm	centimeters
dc	double crochet(s)
FPdc	Front Post double crochet(s)
FPtr	Front Post treble crochet(s)
hdc	half double crochet(s)
mm	millimeters
Rnd(s)	Round(s)
sc	single crochet(s)
sp(s)	space(s)
st(s)	stitch(es)
tr	treble crochet(s)
YO	yarn over

SYMBOLS & TERMS

★ — work instructions following ★ as many **more** times as indicated in addition to the first time.

† to † — work all instructions from first † to second † **as many** times as specified.

( ) or **[ ]** — work enclosed instructions **as many** times as specified by the number immediately following **or** work all enclosed instructions in the stitch or space indicated **or** contains explanatory remarks.

colon (:) — the number(s) given after a colon at the end of a row or round denote(s) the number of stitches or spaces you should have on that row or round.

CROCHET HOOKS																	
U.S.	B-1	C-2	D-3	E-4	F-5	G-6	7	H-8	I-9	J-10	K-10½	L-11	M/N-13	N/P-15	P/Q	Q	S
Metric - mm	2.25	2.75	3.25	3.5	3.75	4	4.5	5	5.5	6	6.5	8	9	10	15	16	19

CROCHET TERMINOLOGY		
UNITED STATES		INTERNATIONAL
slip stitch (slip st)	=	single crochet (sc)
single crochet (sc)	=	double crochet (dc)
half double crochet (hdc)	=	half treble crochet (htr)
double crochet (dc)	=	treble crochet (tr)
treble crochet (tr)	=	double treble crochet (dtr)
double treble crochet (dtr)	=	triple treble crochet (ttr)
triple treble crochet (tr tr)	=	quadruple treble crochet (qtr)
skip	=	miss

●○○○ BEGINNER	Projects for first-time crocheters using basic stitches. Minimal shaping.
●●○○ EASY	Projects using yarn with basic stitches, repetitive stitch patterns, simple color changes, and simple shaping and finishing.
●●●○ INTERMEDIATE	Projects using a variety of techniques, such as basic lace patterns or color patterns, mid-level shaping and finishing.
●●●● EXPERIENCED	Projects with intricate stitch patterns, techniques and dimension, such as non-repeating patterns, multi-color techniques, fine threads, small hooks, detailed shaping and refined finishing.

Yarn Weight Symbol & Names	LACE 0	SUPER FINE 1	FINE 2	LIGHT 3	MEDIUM 4	BULKY 5	SUPER BULKY 6	JUMBO 7
Type of Yarns in Category	Fingering, size 10 crochet thread	Sock, Fingering, Baby	Sport, Baby	DK, Light Worsted	Worsted, Afghan, Aran	Chunky, Craft, Rug	Super Bulky, Roving	Jumbo, Roving
Crochet Gauge* Ranges in Single Crochet to 4" (10 cm)	32-42 sts**	21-32 sts	16-20 sts	12-17 sts	11-14 sts	8-11 sts	6-9 sts	5 sts and fewer
Advised Hook Size Range	Steel*** 6 to 8, Regular hook B-1	B-1 to E-4	E-4 to 7	7 to I-9	I-9 to K-10½	K-10½ to M/N-13	M/N-13 to Q	Q and larger

*GUIDELINES ONLY: The chart above reflects the most commonly used gauges and hook sizes for specific yarn categories.

** Lace weight yarns are usually crocheted with larger hooks to create lacy openwork patterns. Accordingly, a gauge range is difficult to determine. Always follow the gauge stated in your pattern.

*** Steel crochet hooks are sized differently from regular hooks–the higher the number, the smaller the hook, which is the reverse of regular hook sizing.

GAUGE

Exact gauge is **essential** for proper size. Before beginning your Blanket, make the sample swatch given in the individual instructions in the yarn and hook specified. After completing the swatch, measure it, counting your stitches and rows carefully. If your swatch is larger or smaller than specified, **make another, changing hook size to get the correct gauge**. Keep trying until you find the size hook that will give you the specified gauge.

FREE LOOPS OF A CHAIN

When instructed to work in free loops of a chain, work in loop indicated by arrow ***(Fig. 1)***.

Fig. 1

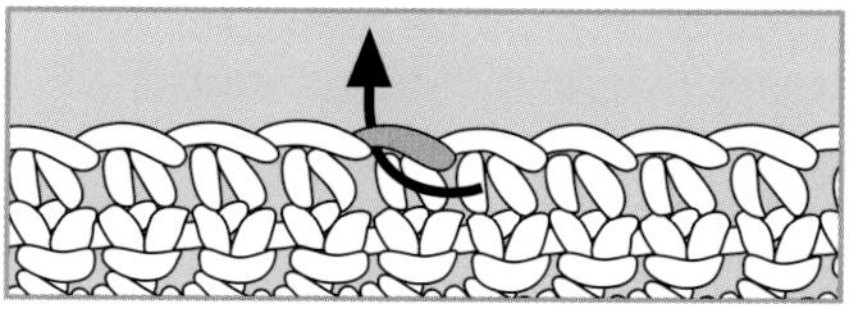

POST STITCH

Work around post of stitch indicated, inserting hook in direction of arrow ***(Fig. 2)***.

Fig. 2

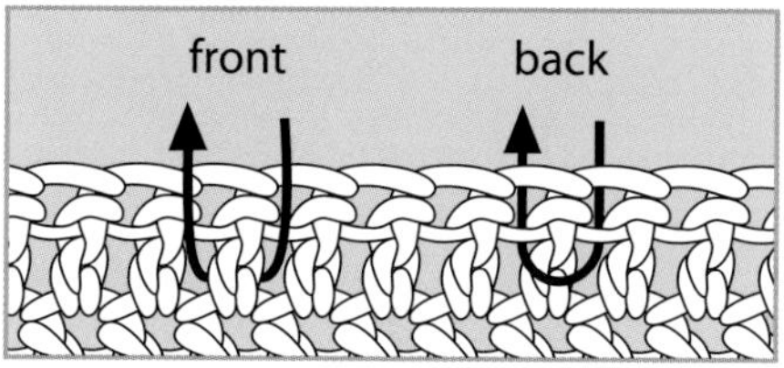

WORKING IN A SPACE BEFORE A STITCH

When instructed to work in a space **before** a stitch or in spaces **between** stitches, insert the hook in the space indicated by arrow ***(Fig. 3)***.

Fig. 3

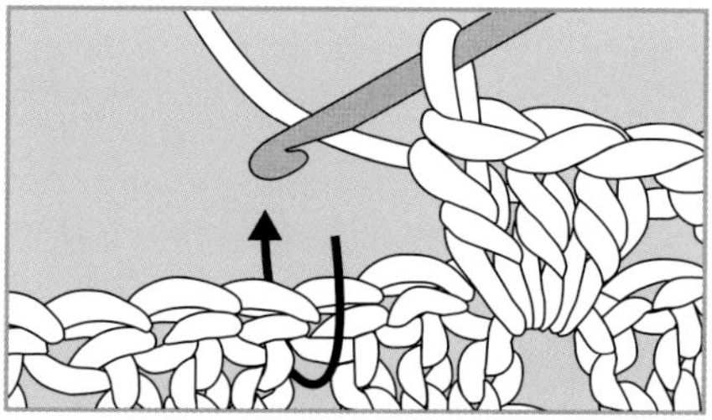

Yarn Information

Each Blanket in this book was made using Lion Brand® Pound of Love®. Any brand of Medium Weight Yarn may be used. It is best to refer to the yardage/meters when determining how many balls or skeins to purchase. Remember, to arrive at the finished size, it is the GAUGE/TENSION that is important, not the brand of yarn.

For your convenience, listed below are the specific colors used to create our photography models. Because yarn manufacturers make frequent changes in their product lines, you may sometimes find it necessary to use a substitute yarn or to search for the discontinued product at alternate suppliers (locally or online).

ARAN APPEAL

#099 Antique White

BOLD CABLES

#148 Turquoise

HONEYCOMB

#158 Honey Bee

WOVEN TREASURE

#133 Creamsicle

We have made every effort to ensure that these instructions are accurate and complete. We cannot, however, be responsible for human error, typographical mistakes, or variations in individual work.

Production Team: Instructional/Technical Editor - Linda A. Daley; Editorial Writer - Susan Frantz Wiles; Senior Graphic Artist - Lora Puls; Graphic Artist - Leia Morshedi; Photo Stylist - Lori Wenger; and Photographer - Jason Masters.